WHAT YOU CAN DO FOR THE ENVIRONMENT

EARTH • AT • RISK

WHAT YOU CAN DO FOR THE ENVIRONMENT

by Mike Wald

Introduction by
Russell E. Train

Chairman of
the Board of Directors,
World Wildlife Fund and
The Conservation Foundation

CHELSEA HOUSE PUBLISHERS

new york   philadelphia

CHELSEA HOUSE PUBLISHERS
EDITORIAL DIRECTOR: Richard Rennert
EXECUTIVE MANAGING EDITOR: Karyn Gullen Browne
EXECUTIVE EDITOR: Sean Dolan
COPY CHIEF: Philip Koslow
PICTURE EDITOR: Adrian G. Allen
ART DIRECTOR: Nora Wertz
MANUFACTURING DIRECTOR: Gerald Levine
SYSTEMS MANAGER: Lindsey Ottman
PRODUCTION COORDINATOR: Marie Claire Cebrián-Ume

EARTH AT RISK
SENIOR EDITOR: Jake Goldberg

Staff for *What You Can Do For the Environment*
COPY EDITOR: Danielle Janusz
EDITORIAL ASSISTANT: Robert Kimball Green
SENIOR DESIGNER: Marjorie Zaum
PICTURE RESEARCHER: Villette Harris
COVER ILLUSTRATION: Bryce Lee

 This book is printed on recycled paper.

First printing

1 3 5 7 9 8 6 4 2

Library of Congress Cataloging-in-Publication Data
Wald, Michael, 1961–
  What you can do for the environment/Michael Wald;
  introductory essay by Russell E. Train.
     p. cm.—(Earth at risk)
  Includes bibliographical references and index.
  Summary: Examines current environmental problems, explores
possible solutions, and reviews recent environmental action and
its effects.
  ISBN 0-7910-1587-4
  ISBN 0-7910-1612-9 (pbk.)
    1. Environmental protection—Citizen participation—Juvenile
literature. [1. Environmental protection.] I. Title. II. Series92-25403
TD171.7.W347 1993   CIP
363.7'0525—dc20   AC

CONTENTS

INTRODUCTION

Russell E. Train

Administrator, Environmental Protection Agency, 1973 to 1977; Chairman of the Board of Directors, World Wildlife Fund and the Conservation Foundation

There is a growing realization that human activities increasingly are threatening the health of the natural systems that make life possible on this planet. Humankind has the power to alter nature fundamentally, perhaps irreversibly.

This stark reality was dramatized in January 1989 when *Time* magazine named Earth the "Planet of the Year." In the same year, the Exxon *Valdez* disaster sparked public concern over the effects of human activity on vulnerable ecosystems when a thick blanket of crude oil coated the shores and wildlife of Prince William Sound in Alaska. And, no doubt, the 20th anniversary celebration of Earth Day in April 1990 renewed broad public interest in environmental issues still further. It is no accident then that many people are calling the years between 1990 and 2000 the "Decade of the Environment."

And this is not merely a case of media hype, for the 1990s will truly be a time when the people of the planet Earth learn the meaning of the phrase "everything is connected to everything else" in the natural and man-made systems that sustain our lives. This will be a period when more people will understand that burning a tree in Amazonia adversely affects the global atmosphere just as much as the exhaust from the cars that fill our streets and expressways.

Central to our understanding of environmental issues is the need to recognize the complexity of the problems we face and the relationships between environmental and other needs in our society. Global warming provides an instructive example. Controlling emissions of carbon dioxide, the principal greenhouse gas, will involve efforts to reduce the use of fossil fuels to generate electricity. Such a reduction will include energy conservation and the promotion of alternative energy sources, such as nuclear and solar power.

The automobile contributes significantly to the problem. We have the choice of switching to more energy-efficient autos and, in the longer run, of choosing alternative automotive power systems and relying more on mass transit. This will require different patterns of land use and development, patterns that are less transportation and energy intensive.

In agriculture, rice paddies and cattle are major sources of greenhouse gases. Recent experiments suggest that universally used nitrogen fertilizers may inhibit the ability of natural soil organisms to take up methane, thus contributing tremendously to the atmospheric loading of that gas—one of the major culprits in the global warming scenario.

As one explores the various parameters of today's pressing environmental challenges, it is possible to identify some areas where we have made some progress. We have taken important steps to control gross pollution over the past two decades. What I find particularly encouraging is the growing environmental consciousness and activism by today's youth. In many communities across the country, young people are working together to take their environmental awareness out of the classroom and apply it to everyday problems. Successful recycling and tree-planting projects have been launched as a result of these budding environmentalists who have committed themselves to a cleaner environment. Citizen action, activated by youthful enthusiasm, was largely responsible for the fast-food industry's switch from rainforest to domestic beef, for pledges from important companies in the tuna industry to use fishing techniques that would not harm dolphins, and for the recent announcement by the McDonald's Corporation to phase out polystyrene "clam shell" hamburger containers.

Despite these successes, much remains to be done if we are to make ours a truly healthy environment. Even a short list of persistent issues includes problems such as acid rain, ground-level ozone and smog, and airborne toxins; groundwater protection and nonpoint sources of pollution, such as runoff from farms and city streets; wetlands protection; hazardous waste dumps; and solid waste disposal, waste minimization, and recycling.

Similarly, there is an unfinished agenda in the natural resources area: effective implementation of newly adopted management plans for national forests; strengthening the wildlife refuge system; national park management, including addressing the growing pressure of development on lands surrounding the parks; implementation of the Endangered Species Act; wildlife trade problems, such as that involving elephant ivory; and ensuring adequate sustained funding for these efforts at all levels of government. All of these issues are before us today; most will continue in one form or another through the year 2000.

Each of these challenges to environmental quality and our health requires a response that recognizes the complex nature of the problem. Narrowly conceived solutions will not achieve lasting results. Often it seems that when we grab hold of one part of the environmental balloon, an unsightly and threatening bulge appears somewhere else.

The higher environmental issues arise on the national agenda, the more important it is that we are armed with the best possible knowledge of the economic costs of undertaking particular environmental programs and the costs associated with not undertaking them. Our society is not blessed with unlimited resources, and tough choices are going to have to be made. These should be informed choices.

All too often, environmental objectives are seen as at cross-purposes with other considerations vital to our society. Thus, environmental protection is often viewed as being in conflict with economic growth, with energy needs, with agricultural productions, and so on. The time has come when environmental considerations must be fully integrated into every nation's priorities.

One area that merits full legislative attention is energy efficiency. The United States is one of the least energy efficient of all the industrialized nations. Japan, for example, uses far less energy per unit of gross national product than the United States does. Of course, a country as large as the United States requires large amounts of energy for transportation. However, there is still a substantial amount of excess energy used, and this excess constitutes waste. More fuel-efficient autos and home heating systems would save millions of barrels of oil, or their equivalent, each year. And air pollutants, including greenhouse gases, could be significantly reduced by increased efficiency in industry.

I suspect that the environmental problem that comes closest to home for most of us is the problem of what to do with trash. All over the world, communities are wrestling with the problem of waste disposal. Landfill sites are rapidly filling to capacity. No one wants a trash and garbage dump near home. As William Ruckelshaus, former EPA administrator and now in the waste management business, puts it, "Everyone wants you to pick up the garbage and no one wants you to put it down!"

At the present time, solid waste programs emphasize the regulation of disposal, setting standards for landfills, and so forth. In the decade ahead, we must shift our emphasis from regulating waste disposal to an overall reduction in its volume. We must look at the entire waste stream, including product design and packaging. We must avoid creating waste in the first place. To the greatest extent possible, we should then recycle any waste that is produced. I believe that, while most of us enjoy our comfortable way of life and have no desire to change things, we also know in our hearts that our "disposable society" has allowed us to become pretty soft.

Land use is another domestic issue that might well attract legislative attention by the year 2000. All across the United States, communities are grappling with the problem of growth. All too often, growth imposes high costs on the environment—the pollution of aquifers; the destruction of wetlands; the crowding of shorelines; the loss of wildlife habitat; and the loss of those special places, such as a historic structure or area, that give a community a sense of identity. It is worth noting that growth is not only the product of economic development but of population movement. By the year 2010, for example, experts predict that 75% of all Americans will live within 50 miles of a coast.

It is important to keep in mind that we are all made vulnerable by environmental problems that cross international borders. Of course, the most critical global conservation problems are the destruction of tropical forests and the consequent loss of their biological capital. Some scientists have calculated extinction rates as high as 11 species per hour. All agree that the loss of species has never been greater than at the present time; not even the disappearance of the dinosaurs can compare to today's rate of extinction.

In addition to species extinctions, the loss of tropical forests may represent as much as 20% of the total carbon dioxide loadings to the atmosphere. Clearly, any international approach to the problem of global warming must include major efforts to stop the destruction of forests and to manage those that remain on a renewable basis. Debt for nature swaps, which the World Wildlife Fund has pioneered in Costa Rica, Ecuador, Madagascar, and the Philippines, provide a useful mechanism for promoting such conservation objectives.

Global environmental issues inevitably will become the principal focus in international relations. But the single overriding issue facing the world community today is how to achieve a sustainable balance between growing human populations and the earth's natural systems. If you travel as frequently as I do in the developing countries of Latin America, Africa, and Asia, it is hard to escape the reality that expanding human populations are seriously weakening the earth's resource base. Rampant deforestation, eroding soils, spreading deserts, loss of biological diversity, the destruction of fisheries, and polluted and degraded urban environments threaten to spread environmental impoverishment, particularly in the tropics, where human population growth is greatest.

It is important to recognize that environmental degradation and human poverty are closely linked. Impoverished people desperate for land on which to grow crops or graze cattle are destroying forests and overgrazing even more marginal land. These people become trapped in a vicious downward spiral. They have little choice but to continue to overexploit the weakened resources available to them. Continued abuse of these lands only diminishes their productivity. Throughout the developing world, alarming amounts of land rendered useless by over-grazing and poor agricultural practices have become virtual wastelands, yet human numbers continue to multiply in these areas.

From Bangladesh to Haiti, we are confronted with an increasing number of ecological basket cases. In the Philippines, a traditional focus of U.S. interest, environmental devastation is widespread as defores-tation, soil erosion, and the destruction of coral reefs and fisheries combine with the highest population growth rate in Southeast Asia.

Controlling human population growth is the key factor in the environmental equation. World population is expected to at least double to about 11 billion before leveling off. Most of this growth will occur in the poorest nations of the developing world. I would hope that the United States will once again become a strong advocate of international efforts to promote family planning. Bringing human populations into a sustainable balance with their natural resource base must be a vital objective of U.S. foreign policy.

Foreign economic assistance, the program of the Agency for International Development (AID), can become a potentially powerful tool for arresting environmental deterioration in developing countries. People who profess to care about global environmental problems— the loss of biological diversity, the destruction of tropical forests, the greenhouse effect, the impoverishment of the marine environment, and so on—should be strong supporters of foreign aid planning and the principles of sustainable development urged by the World Commission on Environment and Development, the "Brundtland Commission."

If sustainability is to be the underlying element of overseas assistance programs, so too must it be a guiding principle in people's practices at home. Too often we think of sustainable development only in terms of the resources of other countries. We have much that we can and should be doing to promote long-term sustainability in our own resource management. The conflict over our own rainforests, the old growth forests of the Pacific Northwest, illustrates this point.

The decade ahead will be a time of great activity on the environmental front, both globally and domestically. I sincerely believe we will be tested as we have been only in times of war and during the Great Depression. We must set goals for the year 2000 that will challenge both the American people and the world community.

Despite the complexities ahead, I remain an optimist. I am confident that if we collectively commit ourselves to a clean, healthy environment we can surpass the achievements of the 1980s and meet the serious challenges that face us in the coming decades. I hope that today's students will recognize their significant role in and responsibility for bringing about change and will rise to the occasion to improve the quality of our global environment.

WHAT YOU CAN DO FOR THE ENVIRONMENT

If society persists in making goods that cannot easily be reused or reabsorbed into the cycle of production, this will be the look of the future.

D O I N G   T H E   R I G H T
T H I N G   I S   C O M P L I C A T E D

Considering the poll that had just come out, *Newsweek* magazine columnist Robert J. Samuelson was hardly surprised by the blizzard of angry reader mail arriving at his office in April 1990. That month, 74% of 1,001 registered voters in a nationwide *Wall Street Journal*/NBC News survey said they favored banning the sale of disposable diapers to reduce the amount of trash sent to landfills. Twenty states were even considering imposing special taxes on the sale of disposable diapers or banning their sale altogether. How had Samuelson provoked his readers? A few weeks earlier, he had written a column defending his family's decision to use disposable diapers on his newborn son.

In his column, Samuelson called the rising tide of rhetoric against disposable diapers "alarmist." His research found that disposable diapers accounted for less than 2% of all garbage in landfills across the United States. He argued that although disposable diapers served as an ugly symbol of America's growing dilemma over what to do with its trash, reusable cloth diapers were not necessarily ecologically superior.

"Suppose everyone switched to cloth diapers tomorrow?" Samuelson asked. "All those diapers have to be washed in hot water, which requires energy and generates pollution. For families using diaper services, the diapers have to be picked up and delivered by trucks that burn fuel, create fumes and worsen traffic congestion. By contrast, most disposables are purchased in shopping trips that would be made anyway. The extra effects of higher energy consumption would be modest, but so is the impact of disposables on garbage."

Samuelson called disposable diapers "an instructive metaphor for the exaggerations of modern environmentalism" and concluded that "we all should want to be good environmentalists, but just what that means in practice isn't always easy to say." His point was not so much that disposable diapers were necessarily better for the environment than reusable cloth diapers, but that comparing the ecological drawbacks of the two was not as simple as it appeared. Because his views drew so many negative letters, Samuelson wrote a follow-up column to answer his critics. This time he backed up his opinions by quoting a scientist from a major environmental organization, Allen Hershkowitz of the National Resources Defense Council in New York. "We simply can't say that disposables are terrible and reusable diapers are great for the environment, or vice versa," Hershkowitz said. "Whatever the choice, there are environmental costs."

Between 1990 and 1991, at least two contradictory studies comparing the ecological consequences of disposable and reusable diapers were released. One study by a private consulting firm in Prairie Village, Kansas, found that over the course of a year, disposable diapers consumed half as much energy as cloth diapers, used one-quarter as much water, produced half the air pollution and generated one-seventh the water pollution. The study also found, however, that using disposables produced four times as much trash in landfills. Procter & Gamble, the nation's largest disposable diaper manufacturer, commissioned the study.

A second study by independent researcher Carl Lehrburger found that disposable diapers created three times as much trash as cloth diapers in the manufacturing stage and seven times

The debate over plastic disposable diapers points up the hard choices facing environmentalists—which is worse, adding nondegradable plastic materials to landfills or using more energy to wash cloth diapers and then discharging detergent-laden wastewater into the rivers and oceans?

as much trash after consumers finished using them. Lehrburger's study concluded that on a per-diaper-change basis, manufacturing disposable diapers consumed nearly six times as much energy as cloth diapers. The study found that overall, using disposable diapers consumed 37% more water than using cloth diapers, because so much water was used in the manufacture of disposables. His study also concluded that plastic, pulp, and paper products used to manufacture disposable diapers generated more water pollution than manufacturing cloth diapers. The National Association of Diaper Services, a lobbying group for cloth diaper services, commissioned Lehrburger's study.

Not surprisingly, environmentalists, diaper manufacturers, and government officials regarded neither study as conclusive. In fact, Environmental Protection Agency (EPA) officials decided in 1991 to begin researching the issue themselves. Bruce Weddle, director of the EPA's municipal solid waste division, added another element to the dialogue by offering a *Los Angeles Times* reporter this observation: in drought-stricken regions—California during the late 1980s and early 1990s, for example—disposable diapers might prove more ecologically sound because they would conserve precious water.

Ultimately, the great diaper debate of the early 1990s offered no firm conclusions. But it did illustrate an emerging approach to assessing the ecological consequences of human activities such as manufacturing, food production, energy and water consumption, and land development. It was important to measure *cumulative* environmental damage rather than isolate only the most obvious damage, and it was important to consider the context in which it occurred.

For example, rather than limiting studies to comparisons of whether disposable diapers create more trash than cloth diapers—the point consumers tend to grasp most readily—some studies now also try to analyze the ecological effects of manufacturing, packaging, transporting, washing, and discarding diapers. This approach might reveal, for example, that although it takes less energy to manufacture a paper version of a product than a plastic version, the paper version might ultimately generate far more water pollution. More comprehensive studies would even try to determine whether local conditions such as a drought or air pollution might offset the normal ecological advantages of one product over another.

INDIVIDUAL EFFORTS IN CONTEXT

Some environmentalists are demanding comparative studies that offer the layperson more detailed, accurate information on how to choose ecologically responsible consumer products. Green Seal, a nonprofit environmental group based in Washington, D.C., was formed in the early 1990s with the goal of evaluating the environmental impact of products through their entire life cycles, from the gathering of raw materials to disposal. Green Seal, which proposed charging a fee to companies seeking to have eligible products certified as environmentally sound, released its first set of standards in 1992.

In the long run, some environmentalists contend, even comprehensive environmental product comparisons miss the point by shifting attention away from more basic ways individuals can reduce pollution or avoid producing it altogether. For example, comparing the drawbacks of paper and plastic grocery bags "is a diversion from the real problem," Fred Munson, a solid waste specialist for Greenpeace USA, told a *Los Angeles Times* reporter. "It's not really paper or plastic, it's bring your own reusable bag." Still others believe most of the ecological pointers coming out of such studies, which typically wind up in paperback books and pamphlets such as *50 Simple Things You Can Do To Save the Earth*, *Save Our Planet: 750 Everyday Ways You Can Help Clean Up the Earth*, and *101 Ways To Help Heal the Earth: A Citizen's Guide*, are far too simplistic.

In an April 1990 article for the *Nation*, ecologist Kirkpatrick Sale argued that "nothing less than a drastic overhaul of this civilization and an abandonment of its ingrained gods—progress, growth, exploitation, technology, materialism, anthropocentricity (exalting human beings as the most significant creatures or objects in the universe), and power—will do anything substantial to halt our path to environmental destruction."

Sale cautioned that while he considers measures such as recycling and energy conservation desirable, even if everyone cooperated it would produce only a small effect. For example, he pointed out, if Americans could somehow eliminate all individual energy consumption—primarily home electricity and private automobile use—it would only reduce total U.S. energy consumption by 28% according to 1987 figures.

"What I find truly pernicious about (simplistic) solutions," Sale wrote, "is that they get people thinking they are actually making a difference and doing their part to halt the destruction of the Earth. 'There, I've taken all the bottles to the recycling center and used my string bag at the grocery store; I guess that'll take

Volunteers help to clean up Central Park in New York City—a noble effort that makes people feel good, but are sporadic voluntary projects enough to cope with the vast outpouring of waste created by an affluent society?

care of global warming.' It is the kind of thing that diverts people from the hard truths and hard choices and hard actions, from the recognition that they have to take on the larger forces of society—corporate and governmental—where true power, and true destructiveness, lie."

Sale argued that environmental "solutions" such as recycling might be viewed in another context as an admission of how far out of control the ecological crisis has grown. "We need

REDUCING SOLID WASTE

Each person on the planet produces at least one pound of trash every 24 hours, for a total of more than 5 billion pounds a day. Here are some suggestions for reducing the trash flow.

1. Recycle goods whenever possible.

2. Save jars, boxes, and other containers for future use.

3. Avoid paper products: try reusable substitutes.

4. Do not accept junk mail. Write to The Direct Marketing Association, 6 East 43rd Street, New York, NY 10017 to have your name removed from mailing lists.

5. Donate unwanted items to community groups. These can be found almost anywhere, but if you are having trouble finding such a group try your local church. Many organizations will even pick up your goods at your home.

6. If you can fix an item, do not replace it. This will reduce solid waste and save you money.

7. Swap clothing with your friends instead of buying new things. This can be an easy way to save money and reduce solid waste. Many articles of clothing are discarded simply because they become unfashionable rather than worn.

8. Use old clothes as rags and drop cloths, instead of buying these items.

9. Try to buy used goods such as dishes and toys; this will save money and reduce solid waste.

10. Donate old magazines and books to hospitals and to other institutions that accept such materials.

. . . to think of recycling centers not as the answer to our waste problems, but as a confession that the system of packaging and production in this society is out of control," he wrote. "Recycling centers are like hospitals; they are the institutions at the end of the cycle that take care of problems that would never exist if ecological criteria had operated at the beginning of the cycle."

Brady Bancroft, a researcher at the Rocky Mountain Institute, a nonprofit energy research center in Snowmass, Colorado, agreed that simplistic approaches do not substantially reduce pollution. "You can't just do 101 things and save the environment," Bancroft said in a 1991 telephone interview. But until reliable, environmentally safe energy supplies are discovered, Bancroft argued, "everyone has to be made aware of energy options and their consequences. There also has to be an economic element whereby the apparent cost of each energy option comes more in line with its real cost." For example, a gallon of gasoline typically sold for between $1 and $1.50 in the United States throughout the 1980s and early 1990s. In Europe gasoline cost at least $2 a gallon over the same period. By refusing to bring the market price for gasoline closer to its true environmental costs—preferably through additional taxes earmarked exclusively for improved mass transit and research into vehicles powered by alternative energy sources—the U.S. government has failed to encourage oil conservation.

INCREASING POLITICAL INVOLVEMENT

U.S. government officials, wary of angering voters and crippling the economy, typically hesitate to impose taxes that

A suburban glass-recycling center. In the future, citizens will have to devote greater amounts of time and energy to sorting and preparing their garbage for proper disposal, and this will change their views about the actual cost and convenience of many products.

boost energy prices to more accurately reflect true ecological costs. The government shies away from investing in environmental research, according to the fall/winter 1990 edition of the Rocky Mountain Institute newsletter, in the mistaken belief that solving ecological problems produces economic costs but no corresponding economic benefits.

Many environmentalists believe that in the 1980s, following a decade in which the United States weathered two major "energy crises," the administrations of Presidents Ronald Reagan and George Bush compounded America's energy woes, and implicitly its environmental problems, with their research funding policies. Neither administration offered much support for research aimed at developing alternative energy sources and conservation programs.

In his 1990 book, *Global Warming: Are We Entering the Greenhouse Century?*, climatologist Stephen H. Schneider even accused those two administrations of discouraging research that might have revealed the scope of a potential global warming crisis five years sooner than the late 1980s, when the issue became prominent. Many scientists fear that man-made emissions of gases such as carbon dioxide, methane, and chlorofluorocarbons (CFCs) are trapping solar heat within the earth's atmosphere, slowly raising global temperatures—a trend that threatens to render the earth uninhabitable.

Political scientist William Ophuls has predicted that as the environmental challenges facing humankind grow increasingly apparent, politicians undoubtedly will play a bigger role in allocating scarce natural resources and monitoring, regulating, and extracting compensation from polluters.

The free market economy would require a massive overhaul to accurately reflect ecological costs, Ophuls argued in his 1977 book, *Ecology and the Politics of Scarcity*. "Those who argue for the market as the solution to ecological scarcity are really urging a political solution, for all of these reforms will require explicit and deliberate social decisions," Ophuls wrote.

Logging companies in the Pacific Northwest are fond of using the slogan "owls versus jobs" to make their destruction of forests seem almost a humanitarian activity, but in truth much of the logging now done is mechanized, and even as more trees are cut, fewer people are employed in the operation.

Current and future generations are in the unenviable position of inheriting an ecological crisis they did not create but must overcome. In his 1990 book, *Green Rage: Radical Environmentalism and the Unmaking of Civilization,* author Christopher Manes offered this chilling warning: "A generation facing a moribund world of ecological scarcity may simply deny social security benefits to an older generation that plundered the Earth and left its children to pay economic and ecological debts." Manes illustrated this scenario with a story about a hunter-gatherer tribe in northern Uganda, a country in eastern Africa.

In the late 1950s and early 1960s, the tribe, called the Ik, was forced from its native lands by the government into a barren, drought-stricken region. Living as scavengers in this mountainous desert, the Ik soon found they could not care for their young, old, and sick. "Ik mothers fed their children for a short time, after which they abused them, beat them, laughed at their injuries, and finally drove them from the family—at three years old," Manes wrote. "The children formed gangs that competed with each other for scraps of food. In the end they had a revenge of sorts. When their parents grew too old to care for themselves, there was no one willing to look after them."

Manes recounted a story by Colin Turnbull, an anthropologist who lived with the tribe, that painted a vivid picture of how far social bonds degenerated among the Ik: "After a raid by a hostile tribe, the Ik decided to flee and build a village elsewhere. A sick old man tried to follow the others as best he could by crawling on his belly. (Turnbull) asked one youth who the old man was. After indifferently stepping over the crawling figure,

This Chicago resident looks askance at a glass of well water after being told that it contains cyanide, a result of the indiscriminate application of agrochemicals to farmland.

the boy said, 'Oh, that's no one, that's my father.' The anthropologist bribed the boy to carry his father, but when everyone started laughing at him, he dropped his burden and went forward on his own."

Manes wondered whether the story of the Ik father offered an example of the fate current adult generations are bringing upon themselves by creating a "biological meltdown" of the earth's ecology. "When various authorities from a variety of disciplines reach similar conclusions about this unprecedented problem, it suggests, at the very least, that the environmental crisis has made our culture obsolescent in ways we have yet to contemplate, with our timid rhetoric about alternate energy sources, recycling, and appropriate technology," Manes warned. "Such is the scope of the environmental crisis that it makes us question our entire history on Earth, back to the origins of civilization."

Paper, not plastic, is the biggest user of landfill space, and it is much slower to degrade than most people think.

S O M E   E N V I R O N M E N T A L   M Y T H S   E X P L O R E D

In 1988, the Mobil Corporation, makers of Hefty trash bags, began selling a new version of the product labeled with claims that it was made of a special plastic that decomposed after 90 days' exposure to "natural elements like sun, wind and rain." Most plastic trash bags in the United States eventually wind up in landfill garbage dumps, where the new Hefty bags, covered by mounds of garbage and dirt, could be expected to linger as long as ordinary bags—probably for centuries.

Mobil was not the first company to market a so-called degradable plastic trash bag, but it was probably the biggest manufacturer to do so, company spokesman John Lord recalled in a July 1991 telephone interview. Consequently, the Hefty bags attracted plenty of attention from consumers and environmentalists. Despite previous company statements suggesting that such a product was impractical, Mobil, recognizing that "biodegradable," "recyclable," "compostable," and "photodegradable" were the hot new advertising buzzwords, wanted a piece of the action. "We said publicly time and time again that we did not think degradable trash bags were the way to go," Lord explained. "But we felt compelled to sell them for competitive reasons. Consumers were clearly voting at the checkout counter for products that were degradable." Apparently consumers did not realize that no such product truly existed.

Mobil never explicitly claimed that the new Hefty bags would decompose faster than ordinary plastic trash bags in garbage landfills. But consumers apparently were not attuned to the nuances of Hefty's claims, since they "seemed to be responding positively to the new bags," Lord said. When an investigation by Greenpeace found no evidence that even the basic "degradability" claims on Hefty's packaging were true, however, officials in seven states sued Mobil, accusing the oil giant of using false and misleading advertising.

By March 1990, Mobil had offered to stop labeling the bags as "degradable," but it stopped short of recalling inventory from store shelves. Between June 1990 and June 1991, Mobil settled with all seven states, agreeing to pay a total of $165,000 earmarked for "cooperative efforts with the Federal Trade Commission to develop uniform standards" for green marketing (advertising that highlights the environmental benefits of products), Lord said.

By the late 1980s, Americans were displaying an unprecedented concern for ecological issues but not a great deal of savvy. Mobil's experience with Hefty bags suggested consumers were so eager for ecologically benign products that they would respond to any seemingly plausible environmental advertising claim.

In July 1991, the Federal Trade Commission (FTC) opened hearings aimed at developing environmental advertising standards after receiving a report in May from a coalition of attorneys general in 11 states. The report assailed advertisers for employing ill-defined claims such as "safe for the environment" and "environmentally friendly" without scientifically substantiating them. But the prospect of government-regulated environmental advertising guidelines hardly reassured groups such as Greenpeace, which had long accused government and business leaders of propagating an ecological mythology far more insidious than anything Madison Avenue had ever dreamed up: risk assessment.

DEFINING RISK

When government, military, and corporate leaders need to define acceptable levels of human exposure to radiation, toxic chemicals, and other environmental menaces, they often turn to a method called risk assessment. Contrary to the public's assumption that risks are calculated solely on the basis of laboratory data and scientific studies that determine risks to human health, legal definitions of what is "safe" frequently rely on factors such as economics, arbitrary guesswork, and the subjective values of the risk assessor.

"In their worst form, risk assessments are tools that industry and government use to disempower and confuse the public," reporter Joann Gutin wrote in the March/April 1991 edition of *Greenpeace* magazine. As an example, she cited the EPA's discovery in the late 1980s that a large proportion of the nation's municipal water systems would not meet the agency's 1984 safety standards for arsenic, a poisonous chemical element, in drinking water. EPA officials calculated that it would cost billions of dollars to correct the problem. In 1988, the EPA quietly eased its standards, allowing higher levels of arsenic in municipal drinking water. Asked about the change, EPA officials announced that a new scientific study had revealed only one-tenth the cancer risk from arsenic, compared to the data used to set the agency's 1984 standard.

Gutin questioned the validity of the new standard. "When tolerance standards change by an order of magnitude between a pair of assessments, you needn't be a hopeless paranoid to wonder if economics hasn't played a role," she observed. Regardless, Gutin added, the statistical analyst's "assumed human," a 30-year-old male, biased the outcome of the study from the start. "Unfortunately, a toxic exposure that makes the 'assumed human' queasy might cause serious illness in a small child and kill a sick or elderly person," she wrote.

Sometimes safety standards are simply guesses, based on no laboratory data whatsoever. In his 1989 book, *Currents of Death*, author Paul Brodeur described how in 1953 the U.S. Navy set the microwave exposure safety standards still commonly used throughout the United States in the 1990s. A scientist hired by the navy "proposed . . . that a safe level could be set at 10 milliwatts of power per square centimeter of body surface," Brodeur wrote. The scientist "arrived at the 10-milliwatt level on theoretical grounds. . . . Although the 10-milliwatt standard was a thousand times the level of occupational microwave exposure considered to be safe in the Soviet Union, it was adopted as a tentative standard in the late 1950s by the U.S. Army, the Navy, the Air Force, the Bell Telephone Laboratories, and the General Electric Company. By 1966, the 10-milliwatt level was generally accepted as a guideline for occupational exposure by the

On the first Earth Day, in 1970, the citizens of Jamestown, New York, dramatically demonstrated how much dirt, dust, and industrial particulate matter falls on each square mile of their city every month by assembling a 30-ton mound of the stuff on their main street.

electronics industry and by most federal and state health agencies."

In 1979, however, a study found that laboratory rats exposed to maximum "safe" levels of microwave radiation developed a statistically significant number of cancerous tumors. U.S. government and military officials managed to suppress this and other microwave radiation health studies, Brodeur wrote, until the mid-1980s.

IGNORANCE AND POLITICS

It is difficult for scientists to calculate risk when dealing with untested chemicals or technologies. Of the thousands of chemicals in common use throughout the United States, only a handful have been thoroughly tested for their effects on humans. Even the effects of many tested substances, when mixed with each other, are not known. Thousands of new technologies simply have not been around long enough for scientists to fully measure their environmental impact.

For example, global warming did not emerge as a pressing environmental concern until the late 1970s. The main reason, author Stephen Schneider explained in *Global Warming: Are We Entering the Greenhouse Century?*, is that although systematic recording of global temperatures began a century ago, the accuracy of much of the data was suspect. Global temperature records were not continuous because measurement sites typically moved from city centers to airports. Even when measurement sites remained in city centers, local heat sources such as subways and skyscrapers probably tainted some readings.

As a result, many scientists have been reluctant to publicly endorse studies suggesting that global warming has begun already.

In the early 1980s, President Ronald Reagan's administration steadfastly opposed increased funding for global warming research. This policy stemmed not only from the administration's hostility toward environmentalists, Schneider suggested, but also from fears that scientists might conclusively prove that global warming required immediate attention—and therefore, the kind of massive government spending that Reagan abhorred. The Reagan administration, hiding behind its voter "mandate" to slash taxes, managed to stall funding for global warming research until 1986.

Politicians have frequently taken advantage of economic and political conditions and voters' fears to shift attention away from ecological issues and to propagate the notion that environmental controls are simply unaffordable. For example, U.S. automobile manufacturers complained throughout the 1980s that increasingly strict fuel economy and pollutant emissions standards hampered their ability to compete against foreign automobiles. Repeatedly, automobile makers have successfully lobbied for more time to meet fuel-economy and emissions standards, arguing that without relief, they would be forced to shut down factories and lay off workers, actions sure to send shock waves throughout the U.S. economy.

Legislators, always mindful of future reelection campaigns, have repeatedly caved in to the automobile industry, reasoning that most voters respond more readily to a healthy economy than to relatively difficult-to-detect improvements in environmental quality. In the early 1990s, many politicians

The United States has more car owners and more cars per person than any other country in the world. The automobile is a leading source of air pollution and toxic waste, and its manufacture uses great amounts of energy and natural resources. Here are some ways automobile owners can conserve energy and prolong the life of their cars.

1. Choose a car carefully. They are many consumer guides that can help you choose a car that is both energy efficient and built to last.

2. Avoid buying optional equipment. Optional items use energy and add to the weight of your car, causing the engine to work harder and the parts to wear faster.

3. Keep your car in good working order with frequent maintenance checks and tune-ups. This will save gas and keep your car running longer. You may decide to learn how to do simple main- tenance yourself.

4. Use unleaded gas if possible.

5. Use radial tires and keep them properly inflated.

6. Do not use your car to store things. Remove unnecessary items from the car. The lighter the car is, the less fuel will be consumed and the longer it will last.

7. Drive smoothly. Frequent starts and stops use fuel and wear car parts.

8. Avoid short car trips if possible. If you do not plan on carrying much, take your bicycle instead, or walk.

9. Seek alternate sources of transportation: trains, buses, bicycles, walking. Consider carpooling if you commute to work.

10. Avoid city driving. Aside from the headache, this wastes energy and time and contributes to urban air pollution.

continued stalling on pledges to protect the environment by depicting environmental legislation such as the Clean Air Act as unaffordable luxuries.

Ultimately, most public misconceptions about environmental issues stem from the refusal of government and business leaders to confront ecological problems candidly, promptly, and effectively. But environmental activists sometimes confuse the public by devoting disproportionate efforts to problems grounded more in aesthetics than in science.

For example, when environmentalists began criticizing disposable diapers in the late 1980s, their message apparently touched a nerve. By 1990, polls showed, most Americans supported banning the sale of disposable diapers, although sales of disposable diapers remained quite strong. But for all the attention the issue received, disposable diapers probably account for less than 1% by weight of trash found in landfills, according to The Garbage Project, a University of Arizona program.

What follows are three examples of Americans' misconceptions about the environment, along with illustrations of how politicians, industrialists, and environmental activists all continue to shape these fallacies, sometimes knowingly and at other times unintentionally. In each case, ecological damage is continuing to mount as government leaders continue to deny the scope of the problem.

THE TRUTH ABOUT TRASH

Perhaps no area of environmental concern breeds as many misconceptions as the nation's garbage problem. Studies have shown that Americans are convinced they produce more trash per capita than any nation, and that disposable diapers, fast-food packaging, and plastics are to blame for straining the capacity of solid waste landfills. American consumers believe that "biodegradable" paper products are preferable to plastic products—a perception many companies have capitalized on by switching to paper or cardboard packaging.

Environmental protesters at the Lincoln Memorial in Washington, D.C. Appeals to save the world's rainforests are often motivated by the highest sentiments but fail to acknowledge the severe economic problems confronting the poorer nations that exploit these forests.

In the late 1980s, however, a two-year study by The Garbage Project cast a new light on these assumptions. For example, The Garbage Project compared typical American and Mexican home trash-disposal habits and concluded that American households produce one-third less garbage. "The reason for the relatively favorable U.S. showing is packaging," William L. Rathje, the professor who directed the study, explained in a December 1989 article he wrote for the *Atlantic Monthly*. "We do not look behind modern packaging and see the food waste that it has prevented, or the garbage it has saved us from making. (Consider the difference in terms of garbage generation between making orange juice from concentrate and orange juice from scratch, and consider the fact that producers of orange juice concentrate sell the leftover orange rinds as feed, while households don't.)"

The Garbage Project also discovered after digging in seven landfills—two outside Chicago, two in the San Francisco Bay area, two in Tucson, and one in Phoenix—that fast-food packaging comprised less than .01% of trash, measured by weight. Overall, plastics accounted for less than 5% of the trash by weight; by volume the figure was 12%. "The real culprit in every landfill is plain old paper—non-fast-food paper, and mostly paper that isn't for packaging," Rathje wrote. "Paper accounts for 40 percent to 50 percent of everything we throw away, both by weight and by volume." The Garbage Project found that telephone books and newspapers comprised between 10% and 18% of the volume of the garbage in the seven landfills studied. "Even after several years of burial (the newspapers) are usually well preserved," Rathje wrote. "During a (1989) landfill dig in

Phoenix, I found newspapers dating back to 1952 that looked so fresh you might read one over breakfast."

Industrialized societies typically deal with garbage by employing four methods used for thousands of years: burying it, burning it, recycling it, or simply minimizing it. Just before World War II there were some 700 trash incinerators in use throughout U.S. towns and cities. But in the 1950s, mostly for aesthetic reasons, municipalities began shutting down incinerators. Instead, they turned to sanitary solid waste landfills—pits lined with clay filters in which garbage is dumped, capped with layers of dirt, plastic, or both, then covered with more trash. In theory, the clay lining prevents groundwater contamination.

Shortly after World War II, civil engineers designed the first sanitary landfills. In an era when the array of pesticides, household cleansers, and automotive fluids now commonly found in most American households did not yet exist, it seemed acceptable, even desirable, to locate landfills along rivers or wetlands. Scientists now regard those places as among the worst sites for landfills because of the high risk that toxic wastes will taint water supplies.

The evidence collected by The Garbage Project suggests that little biodegradation occurs within sanitary landfills, contrary to public perception and the claims made by designers of such facilities. "This may be a blessing, because if paper did degrade rapidly, the result would be an enormous amount of inks and paint that could leach into groundwater," Rathje wrote. "The fact that plastic does not degrade, which is often cited as one of its great defects, may actually be one of its great virtues."

Rathje argued that newer plastics labeled as biodegradable "may actually represent a step backward." When such a

Sometimes a good idea is simple. This modern toilet has a smaller water tank and uses less water with each flush.

plastic degrades—a process that can last 20 years—it breaks into many pieces, but its overall volume barely changes because the degradable component accounts for only 6% of its total volume. The remaining 94% typically amounts to more plastic than if the same item were made of nondegradable plastic, Rathje explained, because items made of degradable plastic are often thicker to compensate for the weakening effect of the degenerating agent.

Even when plastic is incinerated, it may not always be the villain that environmentalists depict, Rathje said. For example, a study by the New York State Department of Energy Conservation showed that the most widely used plastics do not, as some

environmentalists claim, break down into cancer-causing
compounds called dioxins. Even if those conclusions are
debatable, the production of most paper used in the United States
is a more serious and widespread cause of air and water
pollution, since the process emits large volumes of sulfur that
contribute to acid rain.

New home-building designs incorporating active and passive solar technologies seem to promise residents an abundant supply of cheap, clean energy, but are such designs practical for the millions of people crowded into urban areas?

Rather than focusing so much attention on eliminating plastic from the waste stream, lawmakers and environmental activists should concentrate on finding ways to reduce the amount of wastepaper generated by Americans, Rathje suggested. Experts he consulted proposed that freight rates could be changed so it would be cheaper to transport recycled paper than wood for paper pulp, and the federal government, which uses more paper than any other U.S. institution, could insist that most of its paperwork be done on recycled paper.

GLOBAL WARMING ARITHMETIC

Many scientists believe that man-made carbon dioxide emissions must be reduced by between 50% and 60% to stabilize the earth's climate. In the late 1980s and early 1990s, 18 European nations, Japan, and other industrial nations pledged to stabilize or at least reduce carbon dioxide emissions. President George Bush refused at that time to commit the United States to a similar pledge, however, citing economists' estimates that reducing 1990 levels of carbon dioxide emissions by even 20% would cost $200 billion a year.

Energy efficiency experts at the Rocky Mountain Institute (RMI) are convinced that the Bush administration relied upon fundamentally erroneous estimates. Rather than costing the U.S. economy $200 billion a year, reducing carbon dioxide emissions by 20% might *save* that amount, according to an article in the fall/winter 1990 edition of the organization's newsletter.

How did the government and RMI researchers arrive at such disparate estimates? According to RMI, the government based its figures on faulty, overly simplistic assumptions about the costs of cutting carbon dioxide emissions through fossil fuel conservation efforts. For example, the government added up costs associated with fuel conservation measures, but ignored the savings resulting from lower fuel bills. In addition, government estimates of the costs of saving fuel were not based on factors such as buying more energy-efficient cars, appliances, and light bulbs. Instead, the government projected how high energy prices would have to rise to squelch energy demand by 20%, based on decades-old consumer research from an era when "energy savings were far smaller, costlier, and less easily available than they are today," RMI officials noted.

Meanwhile, the newsletter reported, the government has failed to pursue a number of strategies that would encourage major energy savings—and produce corresponding reductions in greenhouse gases—at little or no overall cost to taxpayers. Those strategies include better consumer education campaigns on energy-efficient automobiles, appliances, and other goods; abolishing regulations that reward utilities for selling more energy and penalize them for selling less; and "split incentives" between those who pay for installing energy-efficient devices, and those who use them (for example, offering both landlords *and* tenants incentives for replacing an inefficient furnace in a rental property).

Other measures needed to stabilize global warming include a complete ban on the use and production of CFCs; adoption of farming practices less reliant on fossil fuels and artificial fertilizers, pesticides and herbicides; and an end to wanton deforestation practices both in the United States and abroad. According to RMI research, "over half of global warming can be abated by energy efficiency" using existing technologies at little or no overall cost to the economy. Yet in the early 1990s the Bush administration adamantly dismissed efforts to cut greenhouse gas emissions further, arguing that the U.S. economy could not absorb the costs of cutting fuel consumption and developing technologies to achieve that end.

HOW TO BECOME A GREEN SHOPPER

Packaging materials account for approximately 50% of all the paper products produced in the United States, 90% of all glass, and 11% of aluminum. Reducing the amounts of these materials used in consumer goods will save natural resources and energy and will ease the burden of waste disposal. Here are several guidelines for the consumer.

1. Avoid buying products with excessive packaging.

2. Buy products packaged with recycled or recyclable materials when possible.

3. Buy glass containers rather than plastic ones. Glass containers are easier and cheaper to recycle.

4. Buy in bulk. This cuts down on both packaging and   cost.

5. Avoid Styrofoam and other nonbiodegradable containers.

6. Avoid buying foods out of season. The cost is higher, and the need for long-term storage requires energy-consuming refrigeration equipment and chemical preservatives in the food itself.

7. Avoid the use of electrical appliances and "labor-saving" tools when your hands or nonelectrical appliances will serve as well.

8. Combine shopping trips. This will use less energy.

9. Bring your own bag to the grocery store, and do not accept the paper or plastic shopping bags provided by the store.

10. Avoid synthetic materials. Products made from natural substances, such as wooden toys, wicker baskets, and cotton shower curtains, are safer for the environment.

A SPROUTING
AGRICULTURAL CRISIS

U.S. agricultural methods are widely regarded as the most advanced, efficient, and productive available, and American farmers are counted on to feed a hungry world. Agriculture is critical to the U.S. economy—in the late 1980s it not only produced the bulk of the nation's food but also generated some $40 billion in annual exports, vital to offsetting an annual $100 billion foreign trade deficit. But the soundness of U.S. agricultural methods is illusory because these methods require excessive consumption of energy, water, and soil nutrients, according to John Jeavons, a *biointensive farming* pioneer.

Biointensive farming, like energy-intensive agriculture, also requires water, soil, fertilizer, seeds, and sunlight, but combines these ingredients differently, Jeavons explained in a January 1990 interview with *Mother Earth News* magazine. Like organic farming techniques, biointensive farming shuns the use of petrochemical fertilizers, pesticides, and herbicides.

Unlike organic agriculture, however, biointensive methods focus on cultivating and maintaining nutrient-rich soil as well. On average, U.S. commercial farming practices are depleting soil nutrients about eight times faster than they are naturally replenished; in parts of California the rate is *eighty* times faster. "In the last 200 years, we've lost half our soil base, and that half took 1,500 years to build," Jeavons said.

With biointensive farming, soil nutrients are maintained by a technique called double digging—removing the top foot of soil in a growing bed one trench at a time, loosening the underlying second foot of soil, and then replacing the original

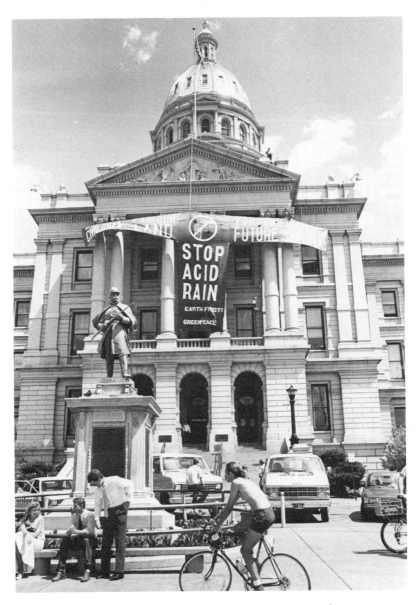

Environmentalists take their case directly to the state capitol in Denver, Colorado, to protest the emissions from a copper-smelting plant.

soil. Double digging is done by hand. By precisely spacing plants and adding *compost* (a mixture of decaying vegetable matter and manure), biointensive techniques help soils retain water (and nutrients that would otherwise be carried away by runoff) and form an envelope of carbon dioxide around a plant's leaves that stimulates growth. Biointensive farming consumes 33% to 96% less water per pound of food produced, no more than 50% of the commercially prepared nitrogen fertilizer normally used, and 1% of the energy of conventional agricultural methods while producing two to six times the crop yield on the same acreage, Jeavons claimed.

By cutting out chemical pesticides, herbicides, and fertilizers, organic farming is a step in the right direction, Jeavons said. But unless it is accomplished using compost derived from the same site where crops are planted, it ultimately depletes soil nutrients as quickly as conventional methods, he warned. Once this depletion of soil nutrients occurs, fertilizers must be brought in from off-site, depleting soil nutrients elsewhere and consuming energy as they are mined, manufactured, and transported.

The potential for biointensive methods to dramatically increase output while farming on smaller plots of land could prove vital to U.S. agriculture. Scientists agree that if global warming is already occurring, resulting droughts could substantially reduce fertile farm acreage and halve U.S. crop yields. A shift to biointensive farming methods would offer the added benefits of reducing agricultural fertilizer runoff (a major source of U.S. groundwater contamination) and slowing global warming by reducing fossil fuel energy consumption.

Even after biointensive techniques are refined to produce dependable crop yields, however, Jeavons acknowledges that

The application of pesticides helps to increase crop yields, but as this picture of empty pesticide tins reveals, they complicate the problem of disposing of toxic waste.

such techniques are likely to face formidable resistance from farmers. In the late 1980s, the average U.S. farmer was 57 years old and generally knew how to grow only one or two crops using conventional methods. Biointensive agriculture depends on frequent crop rotation and lots of manual labor. But in time, Jeavons predicted, biointensive methods would provide the same crop yields, income, and nutrition per labor hour as conventional farming methods—*even though the work would be done by hand on much smaller plots of land.*

If convincing farmers to adopt biointensive methods promises to be a tough sell, convincing the government to accept and advocate these techniques could prove even more difficult. Even excluding the considerable political power of the chemical industry, the U.S. government is reluctant to abandon decades-old agricultural programs. In 1989, the markets for agricultural chemicals totaled some $12 billion, according to Kline & Company, an international consulting firm. Faced with losing these markets, the agricultural chemicals industry will no doubt mount a strong lobbying campaign against any move by the U.S. government to promote biointensive farming methods.

But Jeavons and other agricultural visionaries see no viable alternatives to refining and adopting biointensive farming techniques. "We don't have much time," Jeavons warned. "We need to find out how to grow our food sustainably—without draining any area's resources—over the long haul. . . . It requires diligence and dedication, but in the long run there's not really any other choice."

Long lines of automobiles at these New Jersey gas stations in 1979 were a consequence of political instability in the Middle East. Despite the problems that come with high energy consumption and consequent dependence on foreign oil, the United States still has no national strategy for energy conservation.

chapter 3

THE POLITICS
OF SCARCITY

The United States of America is a nation founded on
the premise of never-ending abundance. American culture is
steeped in the faith that each generation will grow richer than the
previous one. Throughout U.S. history, that conviction has been
rooted in an ever-increasing reliance on technology to fully exploit the nation's immense natural resources. Until late in the
20th century, America's reserves of natural resources seemed
vast and its air and water absorbed damage caused by the exploitation of these resources with little apparent strain.

Since colonial times, the presumption of ecological abundance has served as the underpinning for political and social
values that distinguished American democracy from other forms
of government. The concept of democracy founded on individual
rights predated the British colonization of the New World, but the
abundance needed to support it had never previously existed. The
seemingly endless natural riches of America, however, provided
the final ingredient for a democracy that above all stressed the
right of individuals to pursue happiness (typically this meant
material wealth) as they saw fit.

Traditionally, American democracy has been based on laissez-faire principles: government minimized its interference with citizens' lives and private enterprise. Although the government retreated from these tenets when the nation's economy collapsed during the Great Depression, the administrations of Presidents Reagan and Bush re-embraced laissez-faire ideology during the 1980s, particularly with regard to environ- mental policy making. There was ample evidence by then, however, that laissez-faire democracy was hopelessly inadequate for addressing ecological problems.

Laissez-faire democracy served the United States well for much of its first 200 years. As author William Ophuls states in *Ecology and the Politics of Scarcity*, "American history is but the record of a more or less amicable squabble over the division of spoils in a growing economy." People around the globe looked to America as a land of unparalleled prosperity and political freedom—privileges largely due to conditions of ecological abundance prevalent throughout U.S. history.

By the 1990s, however, it was apparent that America's boom days had long passed—with few exceptions (such as coal deposits), the nation's natural resource stocks were well on the way to being depleted. Technology has offered no long-term substitutes, Ophuls wrote, because so far it "is merely a means of manipulating *what is already there* rather than a way of creating genuinely new resources on the scale" of those discovered in the New World.

As a result, Ophuls believes, the American system of democracy has become an anachronism—a vestige of a bygone era, ill-suited to modern conditions of worsening ecological scarcity. U.S. political and economic ideologies are built on the premise of continued growth that simply cannot continue, because natural resources are dwindling and the environment is fast approaching the limits of its capacity to tolerate environmental abuses. To preserve democratic government, the United States and other western democracies must shift to policies and institutions based on a *steady-state* society that balances a no-growth population, dwindling resources, and nature's waning capacity to absorb poisonous wastes. "How well will a set of political institutions so completely predicated on abundance and molded by over 200 years of continuous growth cope with the hardness, much less the misery, of ecological scarcity?" Ophuls asks.

THE TRAGEDY OF THE COMMONS

When Aristotle once stated that "what is common to the greatest number gets the least amount of care," he could easily have been describing how modern societies treat public resources such as water and air. In "The Tragedy of the Commons," a 1968 article for *Science* magazine, Garrett Hardin credited a little-known early-19th-century disciple of the English economist Thomas Malthus, William Forster Lloyd, with first suggesting the forces behind this phenomenon. According to Hardin, Lloyd wondered why cattle grazing on commonly owned pasture lands were so "puny and stunted," and why the common—the pasture—itself was "bare-worn." Lloyd found that this phenomenon occurred frequently, and he dubbed it the "tragedy of the commons."

In *Ecology and the Politics of Scarcity*, Ophuls described Lloyd's tragedy of the commons as follows: "Men seeking gain naturally desire to increase the size of their herds. Since the commons is finite, the day must come when the total number of cattle reaches the carrying capacity; the addition of more cattle will cause the pasture to deteriorate and eventually destroy the resource on which the herdsmen depend. Yet, even knowing this to be the case, it is still in the rational self-interest of each herdsman to keep adding animals to his herd. Each reasons that his personal gain from adding animals outweighs his proportionate share of the damage done to the commons, for the damage is done to the commons as a whole and is thus partitioned among all the users. Worse, even if he is inclined to self-restraint, an individual herds- man justifiably fears that others may not be. They will increase their herds and gain thereby, while he will have to suffer equally the resulting damage. Competitive overexploitation of the com- mons is the inevitable result."

In modern times, both humankind's reckless exploitation of nonrenewable natural resources such as oil, and its self-destructive patterns of pollution exemplify the tragedy of the commons. For example, when competing oil enterprises drill wells on adjoining properties, each company attempts to extract a maximum yield as quickly as possible or else runs the risk that rivals may pump more than their "fair share" of oil from the pool below. In the boom days of the American oil industry, drillers raced to sink as many wells as possible on properties above known oil pools, creating chaos. In the United States, this kind of competitive exploitation ultimately led to the creation of state regulatory boards that surveyed oil pools and assigned production quotas to competing oil companies on adjoining properties.

Pollution, Ophuls explains, "simply reverses the dynamics of competitive exploitation without altering its nature: the cost to me of controlling my emissions is so much larger than my proportionate share of the environmental damage they cause that it will always be rational for me to pollute if I can get away with it." Some residents of smog-choked cities such as Los Angeles and New York use this rationale to justify driving to work every day even though less environmentally harmful alternatives such as mass transit are available. Typically, individuals reason that even if they stop driving to work, the impact will be negligible because

Toxic waste dumps are an immediate threat to the environment, but cleaning them up means treating the symptom, not the cause. The production of exotic, hazardous chemicals continues, and it will not stop as long as consumers demand more and more goods and services from a high-technology industrial economy.

nobody else will do likewise, and therefore their sacrifice is futile.

While environmental organizations believe that educating the public will encourage environmentally responsible behavior, some studies indicate that this may not be true. For example, studies have found that even the most knowledgeable and concerned advocates of population control do not necessarily practice what they preach. "How reasonable is it to expect from the public at large a sophisticated ecological understanding any time soon, especially since the academic, business, professional and political elites who constitute the so-called attentive and informed public show little sign of having understood, much less embraced, the ecological world view?" Ophuls asks.

CAPITALISM AND ECOLOGY

According to Adam Smith, the 18th-century British economist whose ideas about free-market economics shaped modern capitalism, the "invisible hand" of the competitive marketplace will encourage self-interested participants to unwittingly behave in ways that promote the common good. But ecological scarcity appears to be immune to the benefits of the "invisible hand."

In theory, the supply-and-demand mechanism of a free-market economy sets high prices for scarce commodities, making excessive consumption relatively unaffordable. But in practice, consumer demand for nonrenewable commodities such as oil has proven relatively resistant to price increases, because

Conflicting economic interests often complicate the treatment of environmental problems. Here fisherman Sig Mathisen studies silt and woody debris in the streams of Tongass National Forest, Alaska. The debris comes from logging operations upstream and threatens the local salmon population.

American drivers are far more concerned with convenience and prestige than with how much they pay at gasoline pumps.

Short-term investment strategies are another characteristic of free-market economies that aggravates the modern tragedy of the commons. Since business people see the immediate maximizing of profits as the surest road to survival, investors prefer quick returns on investments to less dependable returns further in the future. Resource companies willing to wait longer for a return

YOU AND YOUR HOME

Many environmental choices you make around your home can actually save you money as well as help reduce environmental degradation.

1. Use mugs or glasses instead of paper cups, and use cloth instead of paper towels and napkins.

2. Keep the lint screen or filter of your clothes dryer clean. This will avoid energy waste, overheating, fires, and damage to your appliance.

3. Install flow-control devices or aerators on your faucets and shower head.

4. Do not leave faucets running, and fix leaks promptly.

5. Water lawns and gardens only in the evenings, when the sun's heat will not cause evaporation.

6. Use chemicals only in well-ventilated areas.

7. Store chemicals and toxic substances in a safe place, with lids and caps on and tightly sealed.

8. Avoid mixing chemical products unless instructed to do so on the label.

9. Look for environmentally safe cleaning products. These are becoming easier to find as the demand for them grows.

10. Use only the recommended amount of laundry detergent. Excess suds make the machine work harder, wasting energy and causing more mechanical problems.

on an investment, as Christopher Manes has shown in *Green Rage*, may suffer for trying to operate in an ecologically responsible manner.

For example, in the western United States, a few farsighted timber companies rejected *clear-cutting*, a logging method that Bob Watson, a timber manager for a southern Oregon mill, told Manes "leaves the forest as bare as a timber yard." Clear-cutting and replacing trees with a managed, single-species forest provides faster and higher lumber yields. But clear-cutting destroys old-growth forests—uncut woodlands with trees of many varied ages—and if carried to extremes denudes the land of trees faster than new trees can replace them.

In the 1980s, "companies that harvested trees on a longer-term, sustainable basis found themselves cash-poor, but rich in assets and thus vulnerable to hostile takeover in the stock market," Manes wrote. "This is exactly what happened to Northern California's Pacific Lumber Company in 1986, when the New York-based Maxxam Corporation . . . took control of the prudent 120-year-old company, financing the takeover with a $754 million junk-bond debt. To pay off the debt, the new company began a massive liquidation of the company's assets—in this case, more than 300 square miles of forest, including the largest privately held stand of *Sequoia sempervirens*, or redwoods, in the world. Some of these trees have stood since the time of Christ, are 300 feet tall, and have trunks the size of a two-car garage. The rush to raise capital has meant the doubling of harvest rates . . . causing alarm even among usually pro-business loggers, who realize they and their community are going to be left without an economic base in 15 years and who lament the passing of the sensible former management."

Another problem with market pricing mechanisms, Ophuls noted, is that although the market responds smoothly when commodities gradually become less abundant, it breaks down when confronted with severe or absolute scarcity. "In such situations (for example, in famines), the market collapses or degenerates into uncontrolled inflation, for the increased price is incapable of calling forth an equivalent increase in supply," Ophuls observes. "In a famine, supply and demand are eventually brought into balance by death (or) emigration . . . not by the price mechanism. Thus the market is unlikely to preside over a smooth and trouble-free transition to a steady-state, for the crisis of

In May 1992, Interior Secretary Manual Lujan faces reporters after the Bush administration overrode the Endangered Species Act and opened a new section of Oregon forest to logging companies.

ecological scarcity involves absolute physical scarcities like lack of food, water, time, or human physiological tolerance for poisons, that mere money can remedy, if at all, only in part (and certainly not indefinitely or all at once)."

Sometimes *low* prices caused by a short-term glut of scarce or finite resources invites ecologically unsound behavior. For example, in July 1991, the *New York Times* reported that a new study showed pre-tax gasoline prices, when adjusted for inflation, were at their lowest levels since 1947. In the *Times* article, David L. Lewis, a University of Michigan Business School professor, suggested that low gasoline prices might inflict long-term damage on the U.S. economy, which had already occurred in the 1970s, by encouraging consumption and allowing Detroit to continue building gas-guzzling cars. Later in the article, Glenn P. Sugameli, an energy specialist with the National Wildlife Federation, echoed those concerns. "If there was a consistent trend toward higher gasoline prices," Sugameli said, "the consumer and auto companies would have a clear signal that more efficient cars is where they should be going."

Finally, free-market economies depend on continued growth, which in turn promotes wasteful exploitation of resources. This is exemplified by the U.S. automobile manufacturing industry, which incorporates planned obsolescence into most of its models in a bid to keep car buyers coming back every few years for a replacement model. Since luxury models offer the biggest profits, the perennially struggling U.S. automobile makers focused on selling inefficient gas-guzzlers even into the 1990s, hastening a time when oil truly becomes scarce and the rate of global warming reaches catastrophic proportions.

Many environmental economists favor restructuring the market by imposing taxes that would force manufacturers to incorporate the environmental costs of production into their prices, and presumably pass these increases along to consumers. But this approach, while potentially useful for adjusting consumption of commodities such as oil, is more difficult to apply to certain kinds of pollution, Ophuls argues. "Some (environmental consequences) can be assigned a price with relative ease—for example, extra laundry bills or house painting attributable to air pollution from a nearby factory," he explained. "However, most cannot be readily quantified—for example, the health effects of air pollution, for it is almost impossible to know who suffers, to what degree, from what amount of which agents."

NO MORE "MUDDLING THROUGH"

In the United States, continuing growth and economic expansion are considered vital in creating opportunities and benefits for the nation's citizens. The accumulation of wealth and large discrepancies in income between different groups is justified on the grounds that the drive for wealth promotes economic growth, and that the benefits of this growth eventually "trickle down" to the poor. Anything that reduces or limits growth also diminishes the flow of wealth through society and increases demands for state-sponsored economic equality. "Since people's demands for economic betterment are not likely to disappear, once the pie stops growing fast enough to accommodate their demands they will begin making demands for redistribution," Ophuls predicted. "If the impact of scarcity is distributed in a laissez-faire fashion, the result will be to intensify existing inequalities. Large scale redistribution, however, is almost entirely foreign to our political machinery. . . . The political measures necessary to redistribute income and wealth so that scarcity is to a large degree equally shared will require much greater social cooperation and solidarity than has been achieved by the system in the past."

As a result, Americans face the prospect of sacrificing some of their cherished individual freedoms. For the first time in American history, government may be forced to set long-term environmental policies that ration resources and manage economic growth rather than rely solely on the marketplace to determine what is produced and how. These developments, Ophuls predicts, will speed the collapse of what he calls "disjointed incrementalism"—decision making based on small, gradual changes in existing policies rather than on radical reforms.

While disjointed incrementalism, more commonly referred to as "muddling through," prevents hasty or irreversible actions on complex issues and promotes decisions that offer almost everybody *some* of what they want, it suffers from serious defects as well. It increases the chances that decision makers will overlook policy options not suggested by past experience. In dealing with new problems such as the ecological crisis, patchwork solutions may be too little, too late. Disjointed incrementalism, Ophuls argues, is ill suited to "any situation in which simple continuation of past policies is not an appropriate response."

The U.S. government's failure to develop a comprehensive energy policy since 1973, when an embargo by Arab oil-producing nations created major fuel shortages in America, probably represents disjointed incrementalism at its worst. By

SAVING ENERGY

There are a number of simple steps you can take that will allow you to save 20% to 40% on your energy costs while helping to protect the environment.

1. Insulate your home. This means the attic, garage, pipes, and water heater. The goal, depending on the season of the year, is to keep the air inside the house either cool or warm, in order to reduce the need for the constant generation of energy.

2. Install storm windows. This will reduce your energy bills and will also help to keep noise out.

3. Avoid the use of air conditioners wherever possible. Fans cost less and do not contain ozone-depleting chloro-fluorocarbons (CFCs).

4. Close off the unused rooms of your home. This will reduce the energy needed to heat or cool the rooms or areas you are actually using.

5. Keep your fireplace damper closed (unless in use).

6. Use fluorescent lights instead of incandescent bulbs. Large companies such as Sylvania, Phillips, and Panasonic are now producing these lights. Even more efficient lights will soon be on the market.

7. Turn off lights when not in use.

8. Use curtains. They keep heat in during the winter and block the sun in the summer.

9. Whenever possible, use cold water rather than hot water around the house.

10. Run your dishwasher only when it is full, or wash dishes by hand.

1991, U.S. oil companies had extended the search for new reserves to previously off-limits sites near pleasure beaches in Florida and California, the wilderness coast of the Olympic Peninsula in Washington state, and inside an Arctic wilderness refuge, all because there was no national policy on controlling the consumption of oil.

"Those potential drill sites, on or near national treasures, force the question of just how far the nation will go to satisfy its oil habit," reporter Timothy Egan wrote in an August 1991 *New York Times Magazine* article. "President Bush has made drilling in

Secretary of Energy James Watkins, President Bush, and Secretary of Defense Dick Chaney at the signing of an executive order in 1991 directing federal agencies to cut energy use by 20%.

Nuclear power plants have proven to be more dangerous and more expensive to operate than planners anticipated, but this does not mean that new technologies will not make them a workable alternative in the future.

the (Arctic) refuge the centerpiece of his national energy policy." But conservation advocates have argued that increasing the average mandatory U.S. fuel-economy standard from 27.5 to 34 miles per gallon by the year 2001 "would save more oil than could ever be pumped from the refuge. But the President will veto any energy bill, according to energy secretary James D. Watkins, that does not include lifting the restrictions on Arctic oil development."

THE INTERNATIONAL
POLITICS OF SCARCITY

Ecological scarcity will fundamentally change politics in the western European industrial nations as well. If anything, western Europe already faces far more serious shortages of natural resources than the United States. Ironically, this disadvantage may offer western European democracies an easier transition to a steady-state society than the United States faces. "Europe has had to contend with ecological scarcity in numerous ways even during an era of unparalleled abundance," Ophuls points out. "Europe has never been as (wasteful) with its resources as the United States. . . . Europeans manage to achieve roughly comparable living standards while using only about half as much energy per capita as Americans. Also, Europeans practice sustained-yield forestry, control land use quite stringently by U.S. standards, and so on. Thus, both because of necessity and because of a generally less doctrinaire attachment to the principles of laissez faire, there exists in Europe a much greater willingness to accept planning and social controls" than in the United States. These generalizations also apply to Japan, which boasts a tradition of self-sacrifice. In the 1970s, the Japanese government conducted a severe crackdown on pollution and instituted strict energy conservation measures.

After years of abusing its environment and natural resources, the former Soviet Union, on the other hand, faces a political transition even more daunting than that faced by the United States. Unlike Western democracies and Japan, the Soviet economy has never flourished, and in the early 1990s it was struggling to provide even basic necessities to many of its citizens.

Offshore drilling operations such as this oil rig in Mobile Bay, Alabama, may increase available oil supplies, but there is a high risk of ocean pollution.

The tragedy of the commons, Ophuls argues, "operates even more viciously in the U.S.S.R. because not only air and water, but virtually all natural resources, are (thanks to state ownership) treated as free or semi-free goods," and "there is an even greater tendency on the part of economic managers to use land, energy, and mineral resources wastefully." The former Soviet Union's attempts in the 1990s to convert to a market economy are likely to make the problem of ecological scarcity worse as the nation cashes in its oil and mineral resources in a scramble to attract foreign investment.

The tragedy of the commons has not progressed as far in China as in the industrialized nations. But that is bound to change as China attempts to industrialize, Ophuls predicts. However, many other Third World nations are in worse shape. Some of these countries, which range from those that are virtually undeveloped to those going through the first stages of industrialization, must cope with ecological scarcity in its crudest form—too many people and too little food—and in some cases, such as Mexico City and São Paulo, air and water pollution more severe than that in fully industrialized nations.

Inevitably, political leaders in the United States, Japan, and western Europe will be forced in the interest of self-preservation to help Third World countries strike a balance between development and protecting the environment. In a 1991 anthology titled *Preserving the Global Environment*, Harvard University demographics professor Nathan Keyfitz warned that "with the whole world under ecological pressure, the disaster that threatens through excessive population and excessive development of the wrong kind is not confined to the poor countries."

The earth as photographed by Apollo astronauts orbiting the moon in 1969. Views of the earth from space have made many people conscious of the fragility of its environment.

chapter 4

A WINDOW OF
OPPORTUNITY

In April 1991, the *New York Times* printed a front-page
story headlined OZONE LOSS OVER U.S. IS FOUND TO BE TWICE AS
BAD AS PREDICTED. The story described a National Aeronautics
and Space Administration (NASA) study that showed that the
earth's ozone layer, which is located in the upper atmosphere
and protects life below from the sun's harmful ultraviolet rays,
was disappearing so rapidly that many scientists had become
alarmed. In the story, EPA administrator William K. Reilly
conceded that vows made 10 months earlier by the world's
industrialized nations to stop producing ozone-destroying
CFCs—chemicals used in refrigeration and air conditioning and
in aerosol can propellants—might "well turn out to be inadequate" by the year 2000.

Michael Deland, chairman of the White House Council
on Environmental Quality under President George Bush, reacted
to NASA's findings with caution. "I think that before we undertake
a major overhaul of U.S. or worldwide policies, we need to very
carefully scrutinize this and other reports to evaluate the accuracy
in a deliberative and comprehensive scientific way," Deland said.

But others, such as Dr. Michael Oppenheimer, an atmospheric scientist at the Environmental Defense Fund, were clearly alarmed. "It means that over the next couple of decades, the level of ozone depletion could border on the disastrous, and it underscores the need to avoid taking risks with global life support systems like the ozone layer and also the world's climate," he warned.

As these conflicting views illustrate, a debate is raging over how quickly the use of environmentally destructive chemicals and technologies must be abandoned, although there is less disagreement that *some* action ultimately will become necessary to avoid irreversible ecological decline.

In *Biodiversity*, a 1988 anthology published by the National Academy of Sciences, Paul R. Ehrlich stated that "extrapolations of current trends in the reduction of (biological) diversity imply (an end to human) civilization within the next 100 years." In *Preserving the Global Environment*, Nathan Keyfitz urged developed nations to act swiftly to help Third World countries break a cycle of poverty fueling potentially calamitous population growth because "a window now open could close within a generation or two." Twenty years earlier, speaking at Northwestern University in 1970, ecologist Barry Commoner warned students that "we are in a period of grace, we have the time—perhaps a generation—in which to save the environment from the final effects of violence we have already done to it."

Has nature already exceeded its capacity to absorb greenhouse gases, or was it just a coincidence that British researchers found that average global temperatures in the 1980s were the warmest recorded up to that point for any decade in the 20th century? Is it true, as Christopher Manes argues in *Green*

On Arbor Day, 1990, artist James Kleveland of Nebraska City, Nebraska, puts a plea for conservation on the side of a barn. Arbor Day is a traditional holiday on which people are supposed to plant trees.

Rage, that the "grace period is over"? Michael Deland, speaking for a conservative presidential administration that rarely aligned itself with the environmental movement, carefully avoided acknowledging the potentially grave significance of NASA's ozone findings. Critics of the environmental movement, Manes observed, typically employ this tactic—denying that an environmental problem exists—even when the best scientific evidence available strongly suggests otherwise.

TECHNOLOGY'S FALSE PROMISE

Confronted with such evidence, critics of the environmental movement typically look to technology for an answer. As of the early 1990s, technology had proven unable to overcome the biggest obstacles to humankind's long-term survival: a looming energy crisis, a population growth rate that threatens to exceed world food supplies, rapidly diminishing natural resources, and levels of pollution that exceed nature's capacity to absorb waste.

A blind faith that technology can save humankind from ecological disaster is hardly confined to conservative critics of the environmental movement. Even some mainstream environmental organizations have advocated exporting technology to Third World countries on the premise that it would stabilize high rates of population growth. Many of these groups also have accepted the premise that averting a full-scale ecological crisis depends on developing a new set of technologies, such as solar-powered automobiles.

Relying solely on technological innovation to prevent an ecological crisis is not realistic, however, considering the time constraints involved. Peter Beckmann's 1973 book *Eco-Hysterics and the Technophobes* is a good illustration of society's overly idealistic faith in technology. "There is little danger from a population explosion in the developing countries, for their population, hitherto kept in check by famine and disease, will stabilize as these countries industrialize, repeating the same patterns as observed in the industrialized countries some time ago," Beckmann declared. "There is no threat of worldwide famine in the near future, because worldwide food production is keeping abreast of population. There is no reason to run out of energy; the Sun will shine for at least another 10 billion years and its energy can be efficiently harnessed. There is little reason to run out of resources, for non-renewable does not mean irreplaceable. Pollution is not an essential by-product of technology; it is an undesirable side product which can be eliminated by more and superior technology."

Nearly 20 years later, these assertions are still commonly repeated by politicians, environmental policymakers, and even environmental activists who insist that technology alone is capable of solving most environmental problems. But in 1990, world population was increasing at an ominous rate, particularly in Third World nations. Parts of Africa were struggling with a decade-long famine, and the Soviet Union was having trouble feeding its population. In California, some of the world's richest and most productive farms were threatened by several consecutive years of drought. The U.S. government had virtually abandoned its 1978 commitment under President Jimmy Carter's

In the heart of Greenwich Village, New York City, a federally financed apartment building employs roof-mounted solar panels to provide hot water for tenants.

administration to develop solar energy technology. And since 1970, average U.S. air pollution levels fell only 14%.

Technological advances ranging from remote sensors on satellites and airplanes to improved computers *did* help document the ever-widening scope of worldwide ecological damage. But new technology offered no corresponding advances toward controlling, much less repairing, this damage. Yet when leaders of the 10 largest U.S. environmental organizations met in 1984 to set a political agenda, the report they produced "portrayed environmental degradation as a technical problem, a problem of resource management," Christopher Manes wrote.

DEVELOPMENT AND OVERPOPULATION

In 1991, a study by the United Nations Fund for Population Activities called *World Population Prospects 1990* found that population growth was about four times higher in less-developed countries than in industrialized nations. About one-fifth of the world's 5 billion people lived in industrialized nations, the report showed. Two years earlier, the United Nations had released a study that revealed a disturbing trend in overall world population growth. Contrary to a widely accepted United Nations projection in 1980 that world population would ultimately stabilize at 10 billion people, the new study showed that if then-current trends continued, the figure would be closer to 14 billion people.

Even the UN's earlier population projection had ominous ramifications, Nathan Keyfitz argued. "In 1950 the world contained 2.5 billion people, and there was little evidence of damage to the biosphere," he wrote. "Now with over 5 billion people there is a great deal of evidence that with another 2.5 billion and continuance of present trends in production and consumption, disaster faces us. The planet cannot over a long period support that many people, yet an even larger number is threatened."

In *Green Rage*, Manes attacked the assumption that stabilizing population growth in less developed countries depends on exporting technology to modernize (and therefore discourage high birth rates in) these nations. "Leaving aside the suspicious fact that technology transfer fits perfectly into the industrialized nations' goal of creating a global market, the strategy has one conspicuous shortcoming: it amounts to ecological suicide," he wrote. "If the worldwide coterie of polluters and mass consumers is joined by Nigeria, Brazil, Peru, Malaysia, and a dozen other Third World countries that retain at least a semblance of their indigenous, Earth-harmonious economies, there is very little doubt that life on this planet will soon become intolerable."

Recognizing this dilemma, environmental groups in the 1980s introduced an innovative strategy for reducing poverty, unsustainable exploitation of natural resources, and pollution in Third World countries: debt-for-nature swaps. Many developing nations are overexploiting their natural resources to meet interest payments on loans from international banks, resulting in reckless damage to irreplaceable ecological treasures such as the Amazon rainforest in Brazil.

In a debt-for-nature swap, foreign governments or environmental groups agree to pay off part of a developing

New Doppler radar systems give weather forecasters detailed informa-
tion about atmospheric circulation that may improve their ability to
predict climate variations in the future.

nation's debt. In exchange, the debtor nation pledges to spend a
certain portion of the money it has saved on local conservation
efforts such as preserving or reclaiming rainforest. International
banks have proven willing to facilitate debt-for-nature swaps
rather than risk the possibility that loans to Third World nations
would prove uncollectible.

When Brazilian President Fernando Collor de Mello
announced in mid-1991 that he would allow debt-for-nature

swaps opposed by the nation's previous president, who condemned them as foreign interference, the *New York Times* raved BRAVO, BRAZIL in an editorial page headline. But some environmentalists recognize that debt-for-nature swaps have limited usefulness. Such trade-offs are similar to other "debt-for-equity" deals in which an indebted nation actually sells off its national assets, or at least control over those assets, in order to obtain debt relief.

BOWING TO ENERGY INTERESTS

After a decade of stagnation, there appears to be a resurgence of the U.S. nuclear power industry in the 1990s, indicating that the federal government is placing little faith (or research money) in conservation efforts or the prospects of developing potentially clean, safe energy sources such as solar power. Not five years after the Chernobyl reactor explosion in the Soviet Union—the worst nuclear power plant accident to date—and 12 years after a near-explosion at the Three Mile Island reactor in Pennsylvania, the U.S. nuclear power industry is reinventing itself as an antidote to global warming.

Since 1974, plans to build 120 proposed nuclear power plants in the United States have been canceled. No nuclear power plant ordered after 1974 ever advanced beyond the early stages of construction. But in 1991, the Tennessee Valley Authority (TVA), a utility owned and operated by the federal government, was lobbying hard to build a new nuclear power plant on the grounds it was "a good, sound, environmental decision," in the words of TVA chief Dan Nauman. No other U.S. utility, public or private, was seeking to build a nuclear power plant at the time, and the federal government hoped a new TVA plant would provide a showcase for promoting nuclear energy as an alternative to greenhouse gas–producing fossil fuels.

In Franklin County, Massachusetts, this modern Cape Cod–style house uses solar technology to provide warmth, air conditioning, and hot water.

*In front of the Lincoln Memorial in Washington, D.C., government offi-
cials inspect the GM Sunraycer, an experimental vehicle powered by
photovoltaic cells.*

With regard to safety, little about the nuclear power
industry had changed since the 1970s. Alvin Weinberg, former
director of the U.S. Atomic Energy Commission's Oak Ridge
National Laboratory in Tennessee, conceded in 1972 that "in
a sense, what started out as a technological fix for the energy-
environment impasse—clean, inexhaustible, and fairly cheap

nuclear power—involves social fixes as well: the creation of a permanent cadre or priesthood of responsible technologists who will guard the reactors and the wastes so as to assure their continued safety" over the thousands of years they will pose a radioactive threat.

In October 1990, the U.S. Department of Energy (DOE) proposed as part of a National Energy Strategy (ordered by Bush in 1989 under pressure from environmentalists) what *Greenpeace* magazine writer Daphne Wysham called "a chilling, albeit novel, solution" to the as yet unsolved nuclear waste disposal problem. Under the proposal, the government would turn nuclear waste disposal over to private contractors, which "the DOE happily notes, would reduce government accountability and insulate nuclear waste disposal from budget pressures," Wysham noted. "Though not explicitly mentioned, it would also limit public access to information about nuclear waste by avoiding disclosure requirements faced by government agencies."

Leaving aside hazardous waste, other questions arose about the alleged ecological benefits of nuclear power. A 1991 study by the Friends of Earth showed that increased dependence on nuclear power would result in significant carbon dioxide emissions, the main contributor to global warming, once stocks of high-grade uranium were depleted within 25 to 30 years and wide-scale uranium enrichment processing became necessary.

Why would the U.S. government try to revive the nuclear power industry, which was crippled by the 1979 Three Mile Island accident and which apparently has so many drawbacks? "Part of the industry's political support comes from the central role energy businessmen have played in the Reagan and Bush administrations," *Village Voice* reporter Andrew White suggested in July 1991.

Demands by opponents of nuclear power that the U.S. government develop energy-efficiency and conservation programs instead fell on deaf ears in the early 1990s. According to White's article, by the 1990s the federal government provided more than

The recent United Nations Conference of Environment and Development, also known as the Rio Conference or Earth Summit, sought to achieve an international consensus on strategies to deal with global warming, deforestation, and species preservation.

*This experimental electric car being tested by the Department of Energy
can cruise at 44 MPH. Though it uses no gasoline, oil or coal must still
be burned at a power plant to provide households with the electricity
needed to recharge the batteries.*

four times as much money to nuclear power research as it spent
on studying renewable energy sources like solar power or
energy-efficiency programs.

BUYING TIME

Energy conservation and efficiency programs have
established an impressive record—when they have been allowed
to do so—for saving money without sacrificing service. For
example, energy-efficiency measures instituted in response to the

Tree planting is a useful activity, but it would have to be done on a massive scale to have any real impact on the problem of deforestation.

1973 Arab oil embargo saved the United States approximately $150 billion a year, according to the March/April 1989 issue of *Harrowsmith Country Life* magazine.

Japan spends less than 5% of its gross national product—the sum of goods and services produced annually by a nation—on energy, whereas the corresponding U.S. figure is 10% according to *Harrowsmith Country Life*. "If the United States were to pursue energy efficiency as vigorously as Japan does, it could save $1.3 trillion to $2.2 trillion (in 1987 dollars) over the next 20 years, cutting its oil imports by up to 3.5 million barrels per day and reducing its trade deficit by $20 billion to $40 billion per year," the magazine estimated. "By avoiding the need to build hundreds of costly power plants over the next two decades, investments in energy efficiency would free up more than $100 billion each year for capital investments in other industries, including much-needed environmental projects."

Amory Lovins, director of the Rocky Mountain Institute (RMI), is commonly described in the media as an energy-efficiency "guru," but even he does not regard conservation and efficiency as a panacea for America's economic or energy woes. "You do a nickel's worth of work here and a dime's worth there," he told *Smithsonian* magazine in 1990, "and pretty soon you've got a half-dollar—and maybe your problem's half solved."

Nevertheless, RMI researcher Brady Bancroft argued, energy conservation and efficiency are intrinsically worthwhile goals if only "to buy us time to make a bridge to a future when we can replace all our fossil fuels and nuclear power supply options with environmentally benign renewable energy sources such as wind and solar power." But it will not amount to very much time,

Educating the next generation about environmental problems is crucial. Here Brazilian children man an information table at the United Nations Conference on Environment and Development in Rio de Janiero in June 1992.

warned political scientist William Ophuls, author of *Ecology and the Politics of Scarcity*. "Conservation can buy no more than a decade or two . . . to adjust to radically altered conditions of energy supply," Ophuls wrote. "The only real solution is to begin a transition to a low-energy . . . post-industrial civilization that depends primarily on flow resources like solar energy."

APPENDIX

FOR MORE INFORMATION

Aluminum Recycling Association
1000 16th Street NW
Suite 603
Washington, DC 20036

American Paper Institute
260 Madison Avenue
New York, NY 10016
(212) 340-0626

The Council for Solid Waste
  Solutions
1275 K Street NW
Suite 400
Washington, DC 20005
(800) 2-HELP-90

Environmental Task Force
1012 14th Street NW/15th floor
Washington, DC 20003
(202) 544-2222

Glass Packaging Institute
1122 20th Street NW
Suite 321
Washington, DC 20036
(202) 887-4850

Global Tomorrow Coalition
1325 G Street NW/915
Washington, DC 20005-3014
(202) 628-4016

Greenpeace Magazine
Paper Department
1436 U Street
Washington, DC 20009

Natural Resources Defense
  Council
40 West 20th Street
New York, NY 10011
(212) 727-4474

The Nature Conservancy
1815 North Lynn Street
Arlington, VA 22209
(703) 841-4860

National Audubon Society
950 Third Avenue
New York, NY 10022
(212) 546-9100

National Consumers League
815 15th Street NW
Suite 516
Washington, DC 20005
(202) 639-8140

The Rocky Mountain
  Institute
1739 Snowmass Creek Road
Snowmass, CO 81654-9199
(303) 927-3851

The Solid Waste Composting
  Council
601 Pennsylvania Avenue NW
Suite 900
Washington, DC 20004
(800) 457-4474

U.S. Environmental Protection
  Agency
Office of Drinking Water
401 M Street SW
Washington, DC 20460
(800) 426-4791 (Safe Drinking
  Water Hotline)

Water Pollution Control
  Federation
Public Education Department
2626 Pennsylvania Avenue NW
Washington, DC 20037
(202) 337-2500

Worldwatch Institute
1776 Massachusetts Avenue NW
Washington, DC 20036
(202) 452-1999

FURTHER READING

Abbey, Edward. *The Monkey Wrench Gang*. Philadelphia: Lippincott, 1975.

Attfield, Robin. *The Ethics of Environmental Concern*. New York: Columbia University Press, 1983.

Bramwell, Anna. *Ecology in the 20th Century*. New Haven: Yale University Press, 1989.

Brodeur, Paul. *Currents of Death*. New York: Simon & Schuster, 1989.

Brown, Harrison. *The Challenge of Man's Future*. New York: Viking, 1954.

Cailet, G. *Everyman's Guide to Ecological Living*. New York: Macmillan, 1971.

Caplan, Ruth, and Environmental Action. *Our Earth, Ourselves*. New York: Bantam Books, 1990.

Earthworks Group. *50 Simple Things Kids Can Do To Save the Earth*. Kansas City, MO: Andrews & McMeel, 1990.

———. *50 Simple Things You Can Do To Save the Earth*. Berkeley, CA: Earthworks Press, 1989.

MacEachern, Diane. *Save Our Planet: 750 Everyday Ways You Can Help Clean Up the Earth*. New York: Dell, 1990.

Manes, Christoper. *Green Rage: Radical Environmentalism and the Unmaking of Civilization.* Boston: Little, Brown, 1990.

Naar, Jon. *Design for a Livable Planet: How You Can Help Clean Up the Environment.* New York: HarperCollins, 1990.

Nash, Roderick. *The Rights of Nature: A History of Environmental Ethics.* Madison: University of Wisconsin Press, 1988.

Nicholson, Max. *The New Environmental Age.* New York: Cambridge University Press, 1987.

Ophuls, William. *Ecology and the Politics of Scarcity.* San Francisco: Freeman, 1977.

Scarce, Rik. *Eco-Warriors: Understanding the Radical Environmental Movement.* Chicago: Noble Press, 1990.

Schneider, Stephen. *Global Warming: Are We Entering the Greenhouse Century?* San Francisco: Sierra Club Books, 1989.

GLOSSARY

anthropocentricity   A tendency to assume that human beings are the most significant creatures in the universe and to interpret the behavior of other creatures in human terms.

biodegradable   Capable of being broken down by microorganisms.

biointensive farming   A method of farming that shuns the use of chemical fertilizers and pesticides, focusing instead on cultivating and maintaining nutrient-rich soil by natural means.

clear-cutting   A method of tree harvesting in which an entire stand of trees is removed in one harvest.

compost   Decayed organic matter suitable for use as fertilizer.

conservationist   One who advocates the preservation of natural resources and their protection from exploitation, destruction, and neglect.

deforestation   The process of clearing forests.

demographer   A scientist who studies the characteristics of a human population, such as size, density, distribution, and other vital statistics.

ecology   A branch of science concerned with the relationship between an organism and its environment.

ecotage   Sabotage, vandalism, or other illegal acts aimed at preventing or halting environmental destruction.

environmentalist   One who is concerned with the state of the environment; a specialist in **ecology.**

global warming   Heating of the earth's surface, oceans, and lower atmosphere due to the entrapment of **greenhouse gases** in the earth's atmosphere.

greenhouse gases   Gases such as carbon dioxide, methane, ozone, nitrous oxide, chlorofluorocarbons, and water vapor that, when in the atmosphere, block heat rising from the earth's surface and radiate it back toward the earth. These gases are the linchpins of the greenhouse effect.

green marketing   Advertising that highlights environmental benefits.

habitat   The place or type of place where an animal or plant naturally lives.

laissez-faire   A doctrine opposing government intervention in the economy.

lobby   To promote or secure the passage of legislation by influencing public officials.

old-growth forests   Uncut woodlands with trees of varied ages, full canopies, a large amount of deadfall, and certain species that depend upon older trees for survival.

photodegradable   Capable of being broken down by light.

physiologist   A biologist who specializes in the functions and activities of living matter such as organs, tissue, and cells.

steady-state economy   An economy in which population growth is kept in balance with the availability of natural resources and with nature's tolerance of environmental damage.

Third World countries   Generally, countries that are poorer than the advanced industrial countries.

wilderness   A tract of land or a region, such as a forest or a wide plain, uncultivated and uninhabited by humans.

INDEX

Conversion Table

(From U.S./English system units to metric system units)

Length

1 inch = 2.54 centimeters
1 foot = 0.305 meters
1 yard = 0.91 meters
1 statute mile = 1.6 kilometers (km.)

Area

1 square yard = 0.84 square meters
1 acre = 0.405 hectares
1 square mile = 2.59 square km.

Liquid Measure

1 fluid ounce = 0.03 liters
1 pint (U.S.) = 0.47 liters
1 quart (U.S.) = 0.95 liters
1 gallon (U.S.) = 3.78 liters

Weight and Mass

1 ounce = 28.35 grams
1 pound = 0.45 kilograms
1 ton = 0.91 metric tons

Temperature

1 degree Fahrenheit = 0.56 degrees Celsius or centigrade, but to convert from actual Fahrenheit scale measurements to Celsius, subtract 32 from the Fahrenheit reading, multiply the result by 5, and then divide by 9. For example, to convert 212° F to Celsius:

$$212 - 32 = 180 \times 5 = 900 \div 9 = 100° \, C$$

A B O U T   T H E   A U T H O R

MIKE WALD is a freelance writer and editor living in New York City. He has written for the *New York Times* and the New York *Daily News* and served as head writer of Nickelodeon's "Make the Grade" television game show for two seasons. Mr. Wald holds a bachelor's degree in journalism from Northwestern University in Evanston, Illinois.

A B O U T   T H E   E D I T O R

RUSSELL E. TRAIN, currently chairman of the board of directors of the World Wildlife Fund and The Conservation Foundation, has had a long and distinguished career of government service under three presidents. In 1957 President Eisenhower appointed him a judge of the United States Tax Court. He served Lyndon Johnson on the National Water Commission. Under Richard Nixon he became under secretary of the interior and, in 1970, first chairman of the Council on Environmental Quality. From 1973 to 1977 he served as administrator of the Environmental Protection Agency. Train is also a trustee or director of the African Wildlife Foundation; the Alliance to Save Energy; the American Conservation Association; Citizens for Ocean Law; Clean Sites, Inc.; the Elizabeth Haub Foundation; the King Mahendra Trust for Nature Conservation (Nepal); Resources for the Future; the Rockefeller Brothers Fund; the Scientists' Institute for Public Information; the World Resources Institute; and Union Carbide and Applied Energy Services, Inc. Train is a graduate of Princeton and Columbia Universities, a veteran of World War II, and currently resides in the District of Columbia.